NYDIA VELÁZQUEZ

FIRST PUERTO RICAN CONGRESSWOMAN

Tammy Gagne

PUBLISHERS

2001 SW 31st Avenue
Hallandale, FL 33009
www.mitchelllane.com

First Edition, 2021.
Author: Tammy Gagne
Designer: Ed Morgan
Editor: Morgan Brody

Series: Unsung Heroes of Hispanic Heritage
Title: Nydia Velázquez: First Puerto Rican Congresswoman / by Tammy Gagne

Hallandale, FL : Mitchell Lane Publishers, [2021]

Library bound ISBN: 978-1-68020-677-7
eBook ISBN: 978-1-68020-678-4

PHOTO CREDITS: Design Elements, freepik.com, cover: LUIS ALCALA DEL OLMO GDA Photo Service/Newscom, p. 6 ANGEL LUIS GARCIA/El Nuevo Día de Puerto Rico/Newscom, p. 9 Associated Press, p. 11 Shutterstock, p. 13 akg-images/Newscom, p. 15 Osvaldo Ocasio, p. 17 Bill Clark/CQ Roll Call/Newscom, p. 19 Brian Baer/TNS/Newscom, p. 21 GDA Photo Service/ Newscom, p. 23 Associated Press, p. 27 PerryPlanet, p. 29 Sharon Farmer - White House via CNP/Newscom, p. 31 teresa.canino@gfrmedia.com GDA Photo Service/Newscom, p. 33 Robin Platzer/Twin Images/Robin Platzer/TwinImages/SipaUSA/Newscom, p. 35 Carl Juste/ZUMA Press/Newscom, p. 37 KEVIN DIETSCH/UPI/Newscom, p. 39 POOL/REUTERS/Newscom, p. 41 Erik McGregor/Sipa USA/Newscom, pp. 42-43 Christopher Gregory GDA Photo Service/ Newscom

CONTENTS

CHAPTER ONE

MOST ADMIRED

"Mom!" Diego yelled. "Marisol is watching television." Diego was one of Marisol's three brothers. They all loved telling on her whenever the chance arose.

"It's too early for TV, Marisol," Mom said. "You know the rule is only after dinner."

"But I'm working on homework," Marisol explained. "I'm watching an interview with Nydia Velázquez for my report about the women I admire most."

"The New York congresswoman?"

"Yes," Marisol replied. "I recorded it while I was at school. Did you know that Velázquez was the first Puerto Rican woman elected to the U.S. House of Representatives? She also grew up in a big family like ours. I wonder if her brothers tattled on her, too."

Pasteles are a popular dish in Puerto Rican culture.

"Still," Mom said, "we have the TV rule for a reason. Why don't you see if you can find another interview through an internet search? You can watch this one later." Mom was making her famous pasteles for dinner. This traditional Puerto Rican dish was Marisol's favorite. Her mother always made the best meals, even after working all day.

Marisol switched the television off and opened her school laptop. "I would like to discuss changing that rule while we eat." She then asked, "Have you ever voted for Congresswoman Velázquez?"

"I will listen to what you have to say. And I have indeed voted for her," Mom said proudly. "Her first run for Congress took place the first year I ever voted. More than half the people in our district are Hispanic. But we had never had someone Puerto Rican represent us."

Marisol's mother had always told all her children that they could accomplish anything if they worked hard enough. She was living proof of it. Like many other people in their neighborhood, she had come to New York after growing up in Puerto Rico. Like Congresswoman Velázquez, she had been the first person in her family to finish high school.

Now Mom was a real estate agent. She was especially proud of bringing so many great families into her own neighborhood. Marisol's mother cared deeply about their community. She volunteered at her kids' schools. And she regularly attended city council meetings.

"I think you should run for public office one day," Mom said as she set the table for dinner. "You are very good at arguing points. So, who are the other women you are writing about?"

"The assignment was to choose the three women I most admire. I'm still trying to find the third."

"Who's the second?"

"Velázquez," Marisol answered with a smile.

"Oh? Who is the first then?"

"You, by leaps and bounds."

"That's very sweet," Mom said. "But you still haven't sold me on changing the TV rule."

LANDSLIDE VICTORY

Nydia Velázquez was first elected to Congress in 1992. She beat Representative Stephen J. Solarz, a nine-term Congressman. Velázquez received more than 75 percent of the vote.

As the first Puerto Rican woman elected to Congress, Nydia Velázquez is a role model for young Hispanic woman everywhere.

CHAPTER TWO

2

LEARNING TO HELP OTHERS

Puerto Rico is located in the Caribbean Sea about 1,150 miles (1,851 km) southeast of Florida.

Nydia Margarita Velázquez's life began in the United States territory of Puerto Rico. She was born in the town of Yabucoa on the island in the Caribbean Sea on March 28, 1953. Nydia grew up as one of nine children. The family lived in a small house along the Rio Limon River. They did not have much money. Their father, Don Benito Velázquez, supported his wife and children by working in the nearby sugarcane fields. Cutting the plants was an exhausting job. Their mother, Carmen Luisa, sold homemade pasteles to the other workers to add to the family's income.

11

After a long day of working in the fields, Don Benito would return home for dinner with his family each night. As they sat around the table, they discussed many important political issues. One was workers' rights. This subject hit close to home. The people who employed Puerto Rico's sugarcane workers did not always treat them well. Many of the workers were overworked and underpaid.

These experiences led Don Benito to speak up in public for workers' rights. He would often get the attention of a crowd by standing on the back of a truck and delivering speeches about unfair labor practices. He even founded a political party in hopes of creating laws to protect laborers. He did all of this with only a third-grade education. Don inspired his young daughter.

Harvesting sugarcane is not an easy job. It was made even harder
by the ways that many employers treated their workers.

When she saw a problem, Nydia drew attention to it just like her father did. A story from a 2012 book called *A Latina's Guide to Success in the Workplace* offers an example of her willingness to stand up and be heard as a young person. "In high school I organized my classmates to protest the dangerous and unsanitary conditions at the school. The building was closed and the protest caused the necessary renovations to be made," she said.

Nydia's parents taught their kids that they had a responsibility to help their community. Her father's hard work and activism set an important example. Nydia's mother encouraged her to keep pursuing education. Nydia was a bright girl. Learning came easily to her. She was only 16 when she enrolled at the University of Puerto Rico in Rio Piedras. Majoring in political science, she graduated magna cum laude in 1974. This Latin phrase means "with high honors."

Nydia wanted to help others like her father did.
Getting an education at the University of Puerto Rico
was an important step toward this goal.

SKIPPING GRADES

Nydia skipped three grades during elementary school. Her teachers promoted her directly from first grade to third, from third to fifth, and from fifth to seventh.

One of the ways that Nydia Velázquez knew she could help others was by sharing her knowledge with them. This would lead her to her first career as a teacher.

3

CHAPTER THREE

SACRIFICES AND SERVICE

Velázquez began working as a teacher in Puerto Rico with her bachelor's degree. At first it seemed that her time as a student was behind her. But she soon won a scholarship to attend New York University (NYU). There, she could pursue a master's degree. The idea of moving to the mainland seemed unimaginable to her family. None of them had ever traveled so far from home. Her father hated the idea of Nydia moving so far away. But two of her professors in Puerto Rico convinced him that the opportunity was too good to pass up.

After graduating from NYU, Velázquez returned to teaching in Puerto Rico. But New York and its people had found their way into her heart. In 1981, Velázquez headed back to the mainland. This time she took a job teaching Puerto Rican studies as a professor at Hunter College. She soon realized that she wanted to become a voice for other Puerto Rican people who lived in her neighborhood. She wanted to help her community, just as her parents had taught her to do.

In 1983, Velázquez began working as an assistant to Congressman Edolphus Towns Jr. After working for Towns for about a year, a spot on the New York City Council became available. Velázquez became the council's first female Hispanic member when she was appointed to fill the seat. Although she lost the seat in the next election, her work had gotten the attention of Puerto Rico Governor Rafael Hernández Colón. He named Velázquez the head of the Department of Puerto Rican Community Affairs in the United States. She was gaining valuable experience that she would soon put to use on an even broader scale.

Velázquez's time working with Puerto Rico Governor Rafael Hernandez Colon connected her with other Puerto Rican people living in the United States.

Velázquez decided to run as a democrat for the United States Congress in 1992. Some people thought she was too focused on Puerto Rico to represent the people of New York. But she saw her connections to her home territory as a positive thing. She told the *New York Times*, "I am not going to represent only a Puerto Rican or Latin American viewpoint. I have a very wide perspective on the needs of this district." She won the primary election with the help of not only Hispanic voters, but also many African American and women supporters.

Following the primary, Velázquez made a visit to Puerto Rico to celebrate her victory with family and friends. The people of Yabucoa were thrilled to welcome her. She urged them to tell their family members and friends in New York to vote for her. In November, she fulfilled their well-wishes as she became the first Puerto Rican woman in Congress.

Velázquez did not only receive votes from fellow Puerto Ricans. Other people of color and women of all races supported her campaign with great passion.

LIKE FATHER, LIKE DAUGHTER

When Velázquez visited Yabucoa amid her first Congressional race, she rode through the streets in the back of a pickup truck. Once again, she was following in her father's footsteps. But she was forging a new path for the people of Puerto Rico as well.

Yabucoa would always be Velázquez's first home. But now her home also included the people of New York.

4

CREATING OPPORTUNITIES FOR OTHERS

As the Congresswoman for New York's 7th District, Nydia Velázquez now represented a diverse group of people. The district itself is the only one in the state to include parts of three different boroughs—Brooklyn, Manhattan, and Queens. It is also made up of people from a variety of races, religions, and cultures. In addition to the high number of Hispanic voters, the 7th District includes many Jewish and Chinese Americans. Many of these people had not had the voice they deserved in their own government. Velázquez was determined to change that.

She vowed to put equal rights at the top of her priority list. Although everyone in the United States is supposed to be treated the same, many working class and poor people often face disadvantages. For example, they cannot afford the same education, housing, or health care as people with higher-paying jobs. Many people in the neighborhoods Velázquez represented also dealt with high crime rates.

One of Velázquez's biggest goals in Congress was creating more business opportunities for minorities and women. As part of this effort, she joined the House Small Business Committee. In doing so she became the first Hispanic woman to serve as a ranking member on a full house committee. A great deal of the committee's work focused on creating better benefits for small business owners. These included business loans, tax breaks, and health insurance for both owners and employees.

Velázquez and other Hispanic members of Congress met with president
Bill Clinton in 1998 to discuss issues important to Hispanic people.

Velázquez has been re-elected to her House seat every two years since her first election to Congress in 1992. Since then, she has co-sponsored numerous bills. Among them has been proposed legislation to create affordable housing, protect voting rights, outlaw hate crimes, and lower interest rates on student loans. In recent years, she has focused her efforts on bills for equal pay for men and women and raising the federal minimum wage. Some bills have passed the House and Senate to become law while others have failed. Democrats and Republicans often have a hard time agreeing on many issues. One thing that they tend to agree on, however, is that small businesses are important to the financial health of the nation.

Velázquez has called small businesses the backbone of the United States economy. In a 2018 interview with the *Guardian*, she said, "Every member of Congress can tell you about how mom-and-pops, small manufacturers or the local diner are not just key to growth, but part of local communities' fabric. When it comes to small businesses' issues, these are not Democratic issues or Republican issues, they are American issues."

Velázquez has worked hard for the working class and poor people of New York. She also believes deeply in the importance of helping small businesses.

FUTURE RESTAURANT OWNER?

A reporter once asked Nydia Velázquez what she would do for a living if she became a small business owner herself. She told him that her business would likely relate to food and healthy eating. Both have always been great passions for her.

Velázquez supports LGBTQ rights. She is seen here in 2019 marching in the World Pride NYC Pride March.

— CHAPTER FIVE —

5

ANSWERING THE CALL

Hurricane Maria left Puerto Ricans with severe flooding and dangerous debris such as fallen power lines.

On September 20, 2017, a Category 4 hurricane named Maria descended on Puerto Rico. High-speed winds and drenching rains continued for 30 hours. The storm devastated the small island and its many inhabitants. Nearly 3,000 people died as a result of the hurricane. Many survivors were left without clean water or electricity for months following the natural disaster.

Velázquez was among the first people to join
the recovery effort. She quickly began working
on getting the people the help they needed. But
she and many other Americans did not think
the U.S. government responded to the disaster
as swiftly or as adequately as it should have.

Exactly one year after the storm made
landfall, Velázquez delivered a speech in New
York City. In it she called attention to the fact
that Puerto Rico was still struggling. The island
accumulated a massive amount of debt
following Maria. Velázquez introduced a bill in
the House to eliminate this debt. "New York
shares a unique and unbreakable bond with
Puerto Rico," she said. "Puerto Ricans are our
brothers and sisters. They are family. And New
Yorkers take care of our family."

One of the most important parts of Velázquez's job in Congress is speaking up for people most in need. This is what she did for Puerto Rico following Hurricane Maria.

Velázquez keeps in close touch with the people of her New York district. In addition to speaking with many of them in person, she also communicates with them through Twitter, Facebook, Instagram, and YouTube. She still sees her job as providing a voice for the people. She regularly posts updates to her website in which she urges them to reach out to her with their concerns. "I'm most effective when I hear from you," she said in one such open letter in 2019. "So, please don't hesitate to contact my office with questions, advice or simply to express your opinion."

Whenever she returns to New York from Washington, D.C., Velázquez tries to visit a public school to speak with students. She thinks it is important to share her story with the young people. "I want for kids to know my story," she told *City & State New York* in 2018. "I truly believe I have a story to tell. And in doing so, I could ignite the interests of these young Latinas to know that if they work hard, if they play by the rules, that they can achieve any dream. And that along the way, there will always be help."

Velázquez is seen here in 2016 visiting a school with New York City Mayor Bill de Blassio and House Minority Leader Nancy Pelosi.

AMERICAN PROMISE ACT

In June of 2019, Congresswoman Velázquez introduced a bill to protect immigrants to the U.S. from deportation. She named the bill the American Promise Act.

Velázquez speaks up for immigrants in the United States. She does not believe that undocumented Americans should be deported.

Nydia Velázquez has achieved many important things as a member of U.S. House of Representatives. One of the biggest is paving the way for other Hispanic women to have a voice in U.S. government.

TIMELINE

1953   Nydia Margarita Velázquez was born in Yabucoa, Puerto Rico on March 28.

1969   She enrolls at the University of Puerto Rico, Rio Piedras at the age of 16.

1974   She graduates from the University of Puerto Rico with a degree in political science.

1976   Graduated from New York University (NYC) with a master's degree in political science.

1981   Velázquez moves back to New York to teach Puerto Rican studies at Hunter College.

1983   She takes a job as an assistant to Congressman Edolphus Towns Jr.

1984   Velázquez is appointed to the New York City Council.

1992   She runs for and wins a seat in the U.S. Congress to represent New York's 7th District.

   She wins re-election every two years since that first race.

2019   Velázquez introduces a bill named the American Promise Act.

FIND OUT MORE

Arkham, Thomas. *Both Puerto Rican and American.* Philadelphia: Mason Crest Publishers, 2013.

Cooper, Ilene. *A Woman in the House (and Senate).* New York: Abrams Books for Young Readers, 2014.

Library of Congress. Puerto Rico and the United States. https://www.loc.gov/collections/puerto-rico-books-and-pamphlets/articles-and-essays/nineteenth-century-puerto-rico/puerto-rico-and-united-states/

Nydia Velázquez. Official Website. https://Velázquez.house.gov/

Yasuda, Anita. *What's Great About Puerto Rico?* Minneapolis, MN: Lerner Publications, 2015.

WORKS CONSULTED

_____. "House Approves Velázquez Immigration Bill." Nydia M. Velázquez. https://Velázquez.house.gov/media-center/press-releases/house-approves-Velázquez-immigration-bill\

_____. "Nydia M. Velázquez." Library of Congress. https://www.loc.gov/rr/hispanic/congress/Velázquez.html

_____. "Nydia Velázquez, Biography." Nydia M. Velázquez. https://Velázquez.house.gov/about/full-biography

_____. "Nydia Velázquez's Voting Record." Votesmart.org. https://votesmart.org/candidate/key-votes/26975/nydia-Velázquez/?p=1

Guilbault, Rose and Nevaer, Louis. *The Latina's Guide to Success in the Workplace*. Santa Barbara, CA: Praeger 2012, p. 20.

Lewis, Rebecca C. "Rep. Nydia Velázquez on leading the way for Latinas." *City & State New York*, March 7, 2018. https://www.cityandstateny.com/articles/personality/interviews-profiles/nydia-Velázquez-puerto-rico-latinas-role-model.html

Marks. Gene. "Nydia Velázquez: 'Helping Americans develop skills in demand is a win-win." *The Guardian*, December 13, 2018. https://www.theguardian.com/business/2018/dec/13/nydia-Velázquez-house-small-business-committee-chair

Newman, Maria. "From Puerto Rico to Congress, a Determined Path." *The New York Times*, September 27, 1992. https://www.nytimes.com/1992/09/27/nyregion/from-puerto-rico-to-congress-a-determined-path.html

Velázquez, Nydia. "July Update: A Note from Nydia." Congresswoman Nydia M. Velázquez, July 10, 2019. https://Velázquez.house.gov/media-center/newsletters/july-update-2019-note-nydia

Velázquez, Nydia. "Velázquez Remarks on Puerto Rico One Year Post-Maria." September 20, 2018. Congresswoman Nydia M. Velázquez. https://Velázquez.house.gov/media-center/press-releases/vel-zquez-remarks-puerto-rico-one-year-post-maria

INDEX

ABOUT THE AUTHOR

Tammy Gagne has written more than 200 books for both adults and children. Among her favorites have been titles about people from different cultures with great passion for their life and work. *Nydia Velázquez* is one such book. Others include *Juan Felipe Herrera* and *Sylvia Mendez*. Gagne lives in northern New England with her husband, son, and a menagerie of pets.